The Little Man In the Map

With Clues To Remember All 50 States

Written by
E. Andrew Martonyi

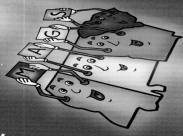

Illustrated by
Ed Olson

SCHOOLSIDE PRESS
SP

Sparks, Nevada

Design and Art Direction
Matthew J. Doherty
Matthew Doherty Design

Editing by Evelyn Hughes
Present Perfect Writing
and Editorial Services

Published by Schoolside Press
www.schoolsidepress.com

Fourth Edition

Library of Congress Control Number: 2006939784

Publisher's Cataloging-in-Publication
(Provided by Quality Books, Inc.)
Martonyi, E. Andrew.
The little man in the map : with clues to remember
all 50 states / written by E. Andrew Martonyi ;
illustrated by Ed Olson.—1st ed.
p. cm.
LCCN 2006939784
SUMMARY: Elementary school children identify the
shapes formed by U.S. state boundaries in this rhyming
story that teaches mnemonic devices for learning the
names and locations of the fifty states.
Audience: Grades 2-6.
ISBN-13: 978-0-9785100-4-6
ISBN-10: 0-9785100-4-6

1. U.S. states—Juvenile literature. 2. United
States—Geography—Juvenile literature. [1. United
States—Geography. 2. Stories in rhyme.]   I. Olson, Ed, ill..
II. Title.

E180.M37 2007   917.3
                                 QBI06-600718

Printed in the United States of America.
Set in Stone Sans, Stone Informal, and Ozwald.

10 9 8 7 6 5

Acknowledgements

Every book comes to life in direct relation to the creative efforts of those involved. I was very fortunate that so many talented and generous people were engaged in this project.

Foremost, I thank my sister, **Enikő Katalin Gellai**, without whose help and encouragement this project might never have been completed. She believed in it from the beginning and was involved in every aspect, giving many hours of her time and generously sharing her talent and creativity.

A very special acknowledgement goes to my granddaughter, **Danielle**. Only five years old at the time, she was "the first to smile at the Little Man In the Map." It was her interest in and curiosity about my travels that inspired me to find an easier way to teach and learn the states. She loved the character of the Little Man, and was the first to demonstrate that the ideas in this book really do help readers remember the states.

I am extremely grateful to the teachers, students, and parents who were involved in testing this concept, and thank them for their many words of encouragement and appreciation.

- **Kathy Moran** (Ann Arbor, Michigan) was the first to evaluate the concept in her sixth-grade class. The feedback from her students and their parents proved to me that there was merit in this concept, both inside and outside the classroom.
- **Kal DePaco** (Santa Clarita Valley, California) and her second-graders turned the manuscript into a play that the kids performed for their school, families, and friends.
- **Gloria Hayden** (Woodland Hills, California) used it in her class even before the illustrations were developed.
   The fifth-grade class of **AnnMarie Robles** (Camarillo, California) showed the effectiveness of the program through their test scores.
- **Patrice Jannace** (Covina, California) used a draft in her fifth-grade class and reported that the kids pulled others into their classroom to show them the Little Man In the Map.
- **Pamela L. Schwagerl**, publisher (Reedley, California), who has homeschooled all six of her children, used the program with her last two daughters, Emma and Sally, who loved it so much they asked to do more than the daily assigned pages.

Many additional thanks to …

My editor, **Evelyn Hughes**, who pushed, prodded, coaxed, scolded, and molded this work to bring it into shape.

My art director, **Matt Doherty**, who was able to see my too-ambitious vision, give it direction, clarity, and focus, and shepherd it to its conclusion.

My illustrator, **Ed Olson**, without whose formidable talents and generous sharing of ideas some of the real magic in this book might not have emerged.

My entire family, whose encouragement and contributions have been immensely valuable and greatly appreciated.

Finally, I thank my wonderful, loving wife, **Irma**. No one has been more supportive. Without that unselfish support, her unfailing love, and her steadfast cheerfulness, this book could never have happened.

E. Andrew Martonyi

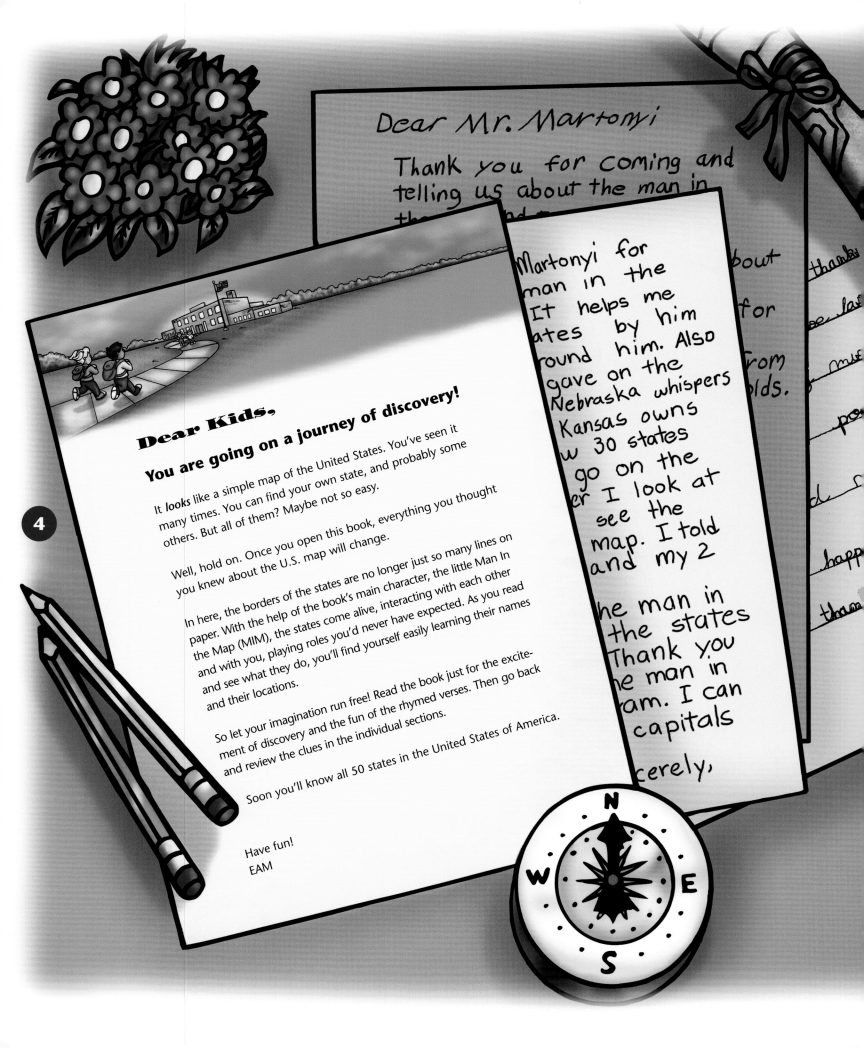

Dear Kids,

You are going on a journey of discovery!

It *looks* like a simple map of the United States. You've seen it many times. You can find your own state, and probably some others. But all of them? Maybe not so easy.

Well, hold on. Once you open this book, everything you thought you knew about the U.S. map will change.

In here, the borders of the states are no longer just so many lines on paper. With the help of the book's main character, the little Man In the Map (MIM), the states come alive, interacting with each other and with you, playing roles you'd never have expected. As you read and see what they do, you'll find yourself easily learning their names and their locations.

So let your imagination run free! Read the book just for the excitement of discovery and the fun of the rhymed verses. Then go back and review the clues in the individual sections.

Soon you'll know all 50 states in the United States of America.

Have fun!
EAM

Dear Mr. Martonyi

Thank you for coming and telling us about the man in

We'll use the clues you locate
And we'll write them
    out in verse,
For rhymes
    are easy to recall
And fun when you rehearse.

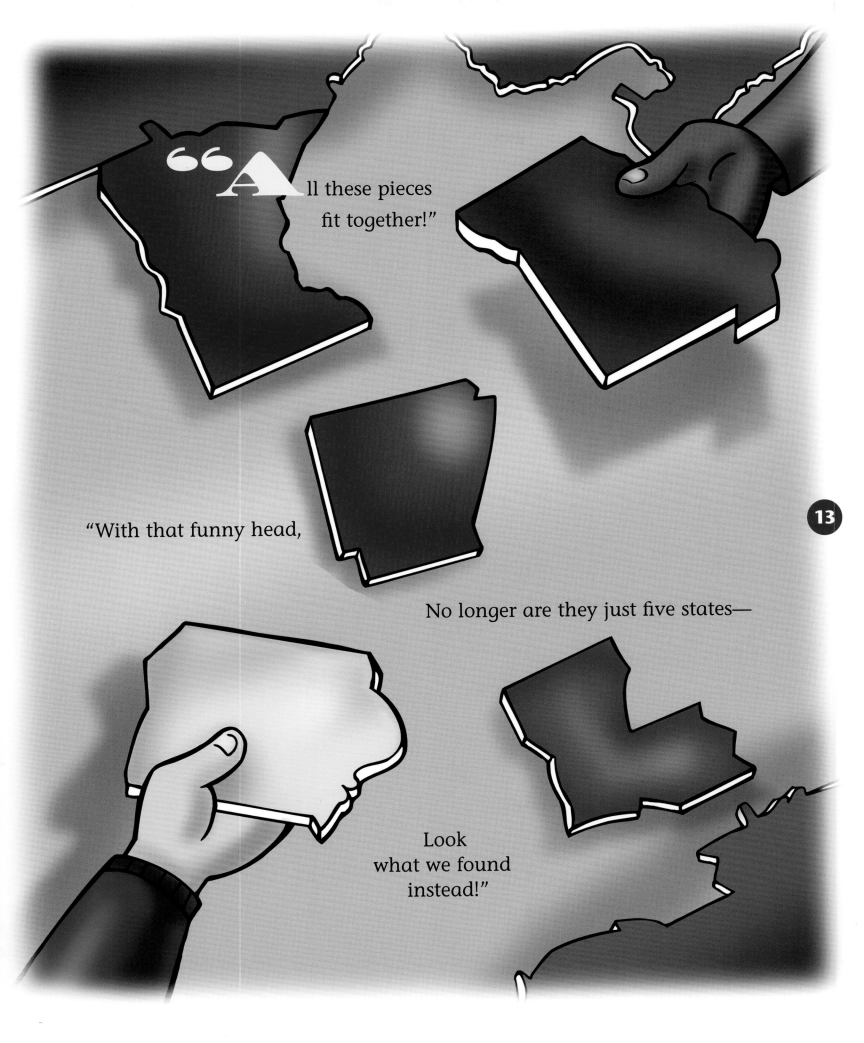

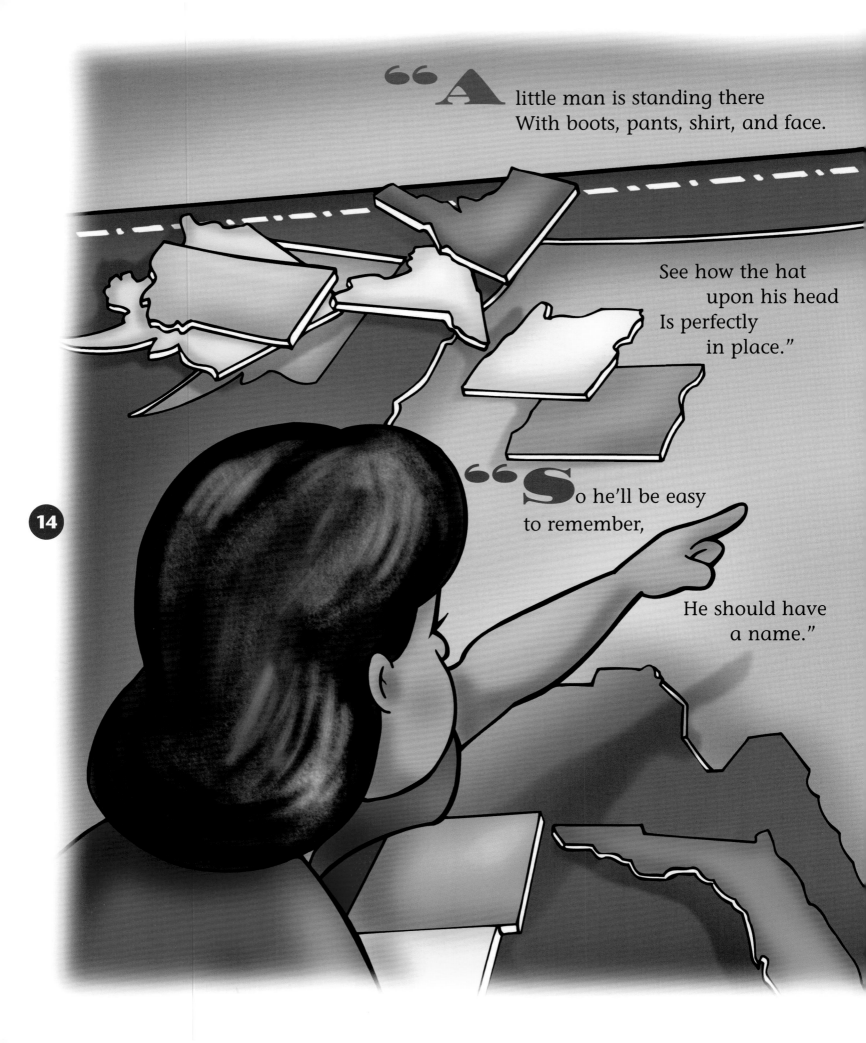

"Let's use three letters
from the states—
The five that
make his frame."

15

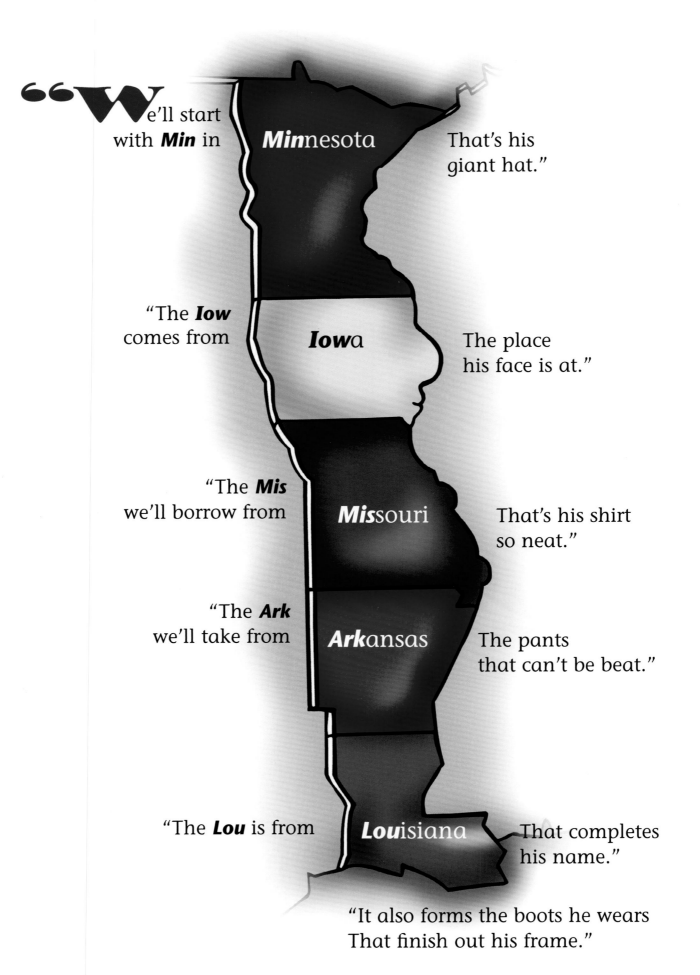

"We'll start with **Min** in **Min**nesota

That's his giant hat."

"The **Iow** comes from **Iow**a

The place his face is at."

"The **Mis** we'll borrow from **Mis**souri

That's his shirt so neat."

"The **Ark** we'll take from **Ark**ansas

The pants that can't be beat."

"The **Lou** is from **Lou**isiana

That completes his name."

"It also forms the boots he wears
That finish out his frame."

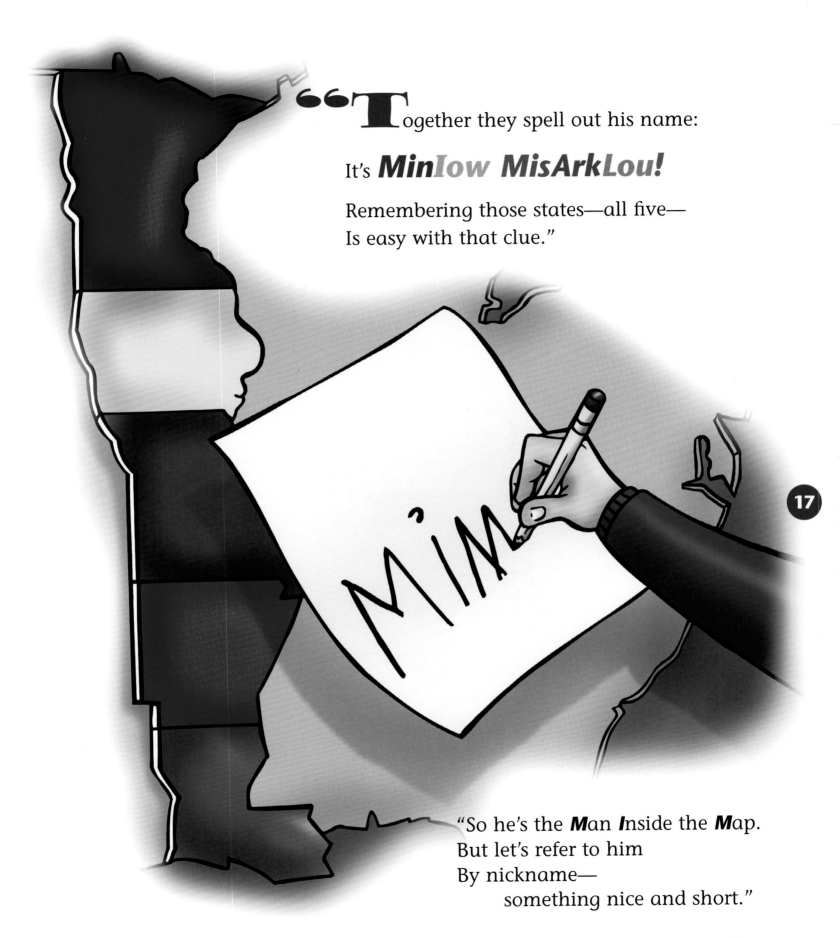

"**T**ogether they spell out his name:

It's *MinIow MisArkLou!*

Remembering those states—all five—
Is easy with that clue."

17

"So he's the **M**an **I**nside the **M**ap.
But let's refer to him
By nickname—
        something nice and short."

"Why don't we call him *MIM*?"

"You

"....Imagination is the magic key

To help unlock the clues you need
To learn geography."

A region at a time's the way

"We'll start with clues
for Midwest states,
Then South, then East, then West.

**Western
States**

That you can learn them best."

Northeastern
States

Midwestern
States

Southeastern
States

South **C**entral
States

Midwestern States   *12 states*

The Midwest region
     has twelve states,
Like members of a jury.
There's Minnesota, Iowa,
And, under them, Missouri;

They're my hat, my face, my shirt,
And then there are nine more:
Five are right in front of me,
In back of me are four.

26

My hat's so tall, it takes two states
To prop it from behind.
So North Dakota stands on South
To keep the back aligned.

Nebraska whispers in my ear,
And Kansas is a pack
Of schoolbooks I can carry
When I strap it on my back.

My eyes look on Wisconsin's cheese
(It makes the very best),
While Illinois leans on my shirt
And honks my nose in jest.

28

Michigan's a giant mitten
In a winter storm.
With Indiana as a sleeve,
The arm beneath stays warm.

Let's not forget that Michigan
Has two peninsulas:
The lower one is mitten-shaped,
The upper one has 'paws.'

That dog in upper Michigan's
A frisky, playful pup.
He grabs that mitten in his mouth,
All set to chew it up.

Ohio is my drinking cup.
It has its own supply
Of water from Lake Erie,
So it never will run dry.

Midwestern States

My hat, my face, my stylish shirt.
Two states that prop my hat.
A whispering state, a pack of books.
Say "Cheese!" A honking pat.

A puppy and a mitten,
With a cozy sleeve below.
My drinking cup's the final state.

Now to the **SOUTH** we'll go.

South Central states are very few.
They number only four:
There's Arkansas, Louisiana,
And, due west, two more.

Arkansas—my pants.
Louisiana—that's my boot.

I think I see a place to sit,
But first I have to scoot
The handle part of Oklahoma
Over just a bit.

Now Texas is
my Longhorn chair,
And it's a perfect fit.

South Central States *4 states*

A boot that keeps my feet so warm.
My chair—a perfect fit.
My pants so nice and comfy,
And that state I scoot a bit.

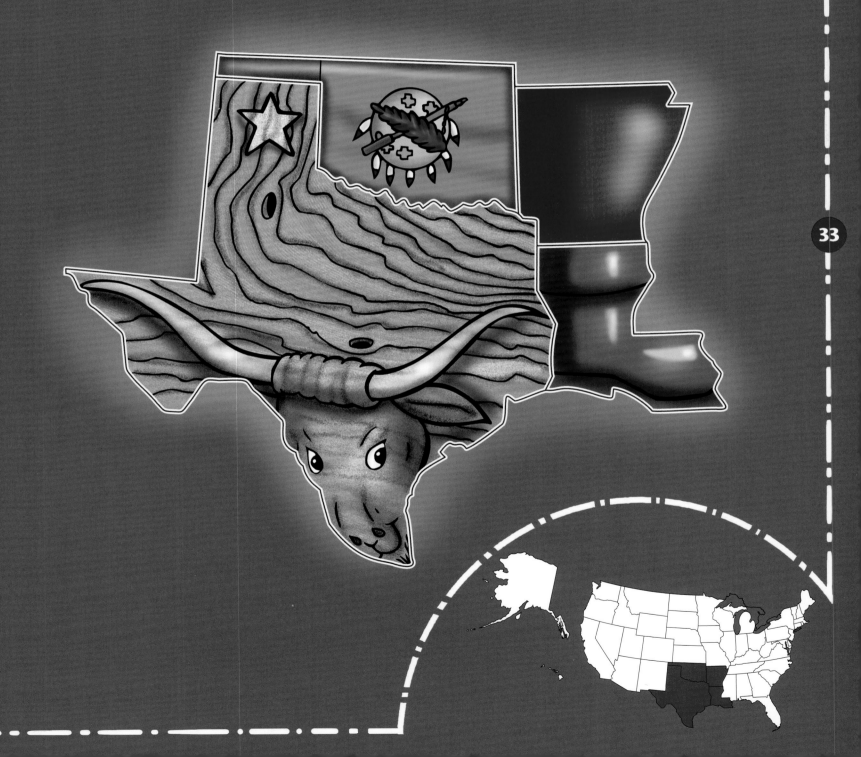

Southeastern States

12 states

Twelve Southeastern states are next.
Now, here is where we're able
To put together six of them
So I can have a table.

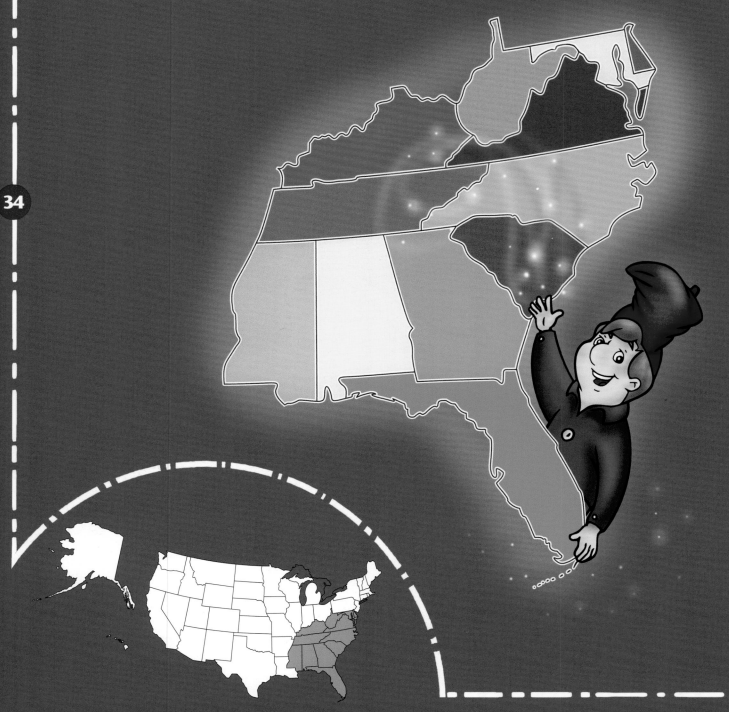

Tennessee and North Carolina
Make that perfect table.
All they need are four good legs
To keep them nice and stable.

Mississippi, Alabama
Boost the western edge.
Georgia holds the middle,
Next to South Carolina's wedge.

Those legs sure need a memory aid,
So MAGS will keep them straight.
We'll think of MAGS and we'll recall
The letter of each state.

Below the A and G of MAGS
(The four legs' middle states)
Is where we spot
        the turtle's head
That Florida creates.

Kentucky bluegrass on the table
And Virginia ham.
For making gravy, West Virginia
Is the perfect pan.

Maryland is steaming gravy
Boiling from that pan.
Luckily, it's mainly spilling
Smack-dab on the ham!

But gravy
splashed
on Delaware!
So here's
another clue:
A washing in
Atlantic waters
Cleans that state
like new.

Southeastern States

12 states

REGIONAL REVIEW

The table top is two states,
And the MAGS (its legs) are four.
One state's below the A and G;
The table holds five more.

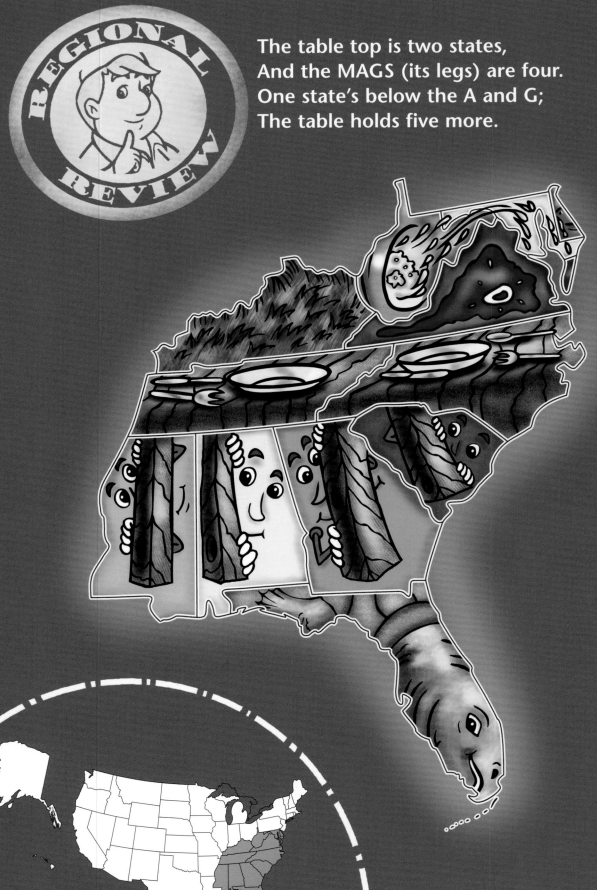

WASHINGTON
DISTRICT OF COLUMBIA

Washington, our capital—
The District of Columbia—
On the east meets Maryland,
On the west, Virginia.

It's not a state or part of one,
This home of U.S. presidents.
George Washington picked out the site
Especially for the government.

39

Northeastern States

Now the clues for Northeast states—
They number only nine.

For the six we call
'New England,'
I've made up a sign.

New England

If we need to find New England
In the dark of night,
We'll reach right up for New York state,
To use it as a light!

You see the switch above New York?
That's Lake Ontario.
Push ON in that 'Ontario'
To make the flashlight glow.

And when we're through,
    we'll put it back
(While flicking off its switch)
On Pennsylvania
    and New Jersey.
That's its storage niche.

I have a boot I use for skiing
Through New England snow.
There! It's Vermont, plus
Massachusetts
With its curvy toe.

42

Should I want
    a platform boot,
Well, I can have that too:
Connect Connecticut
    and Rhode Island
With a dab of glue.

If the boot's a little snug,
Well, here's a nice surprise—
We'll add New Hampshire
   to the leg
To make a larger size.

The V and N are over M,
Which stands on C and R.
Now with that clue
   you'll know how close
Those five pals really are.

43

M

aine's the last New England state,
And farthest east of all—
A clock that's first to see the sun
And first to see night fall.

Northeastern States

9 states

Two states to store the switched-on light
That shines upon a boot
Constructed out of five small states.
The clock the sun salutes.

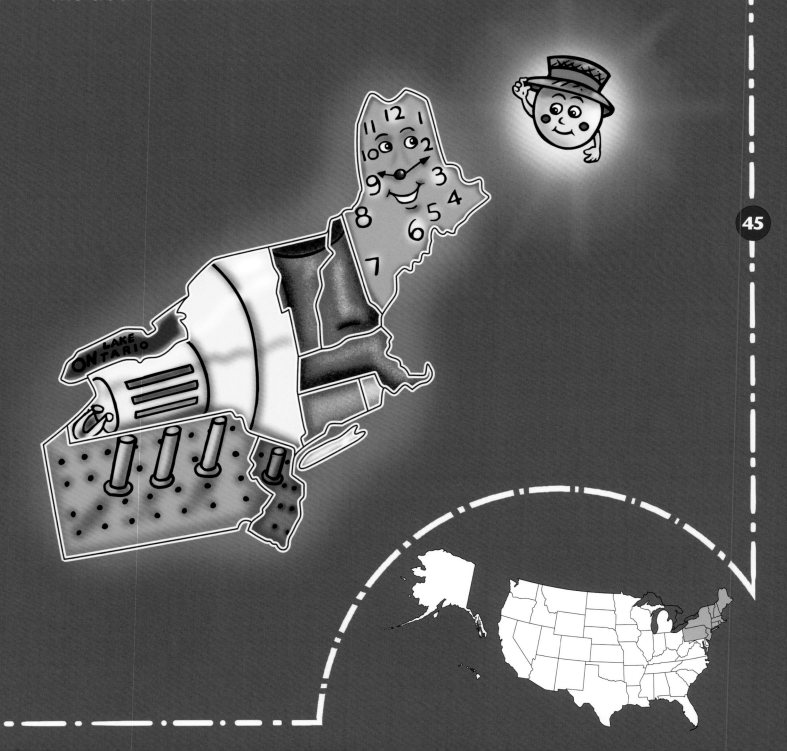

Western States

13 states

Let's head west
to thirteen states
Where we can solve
a riddle:

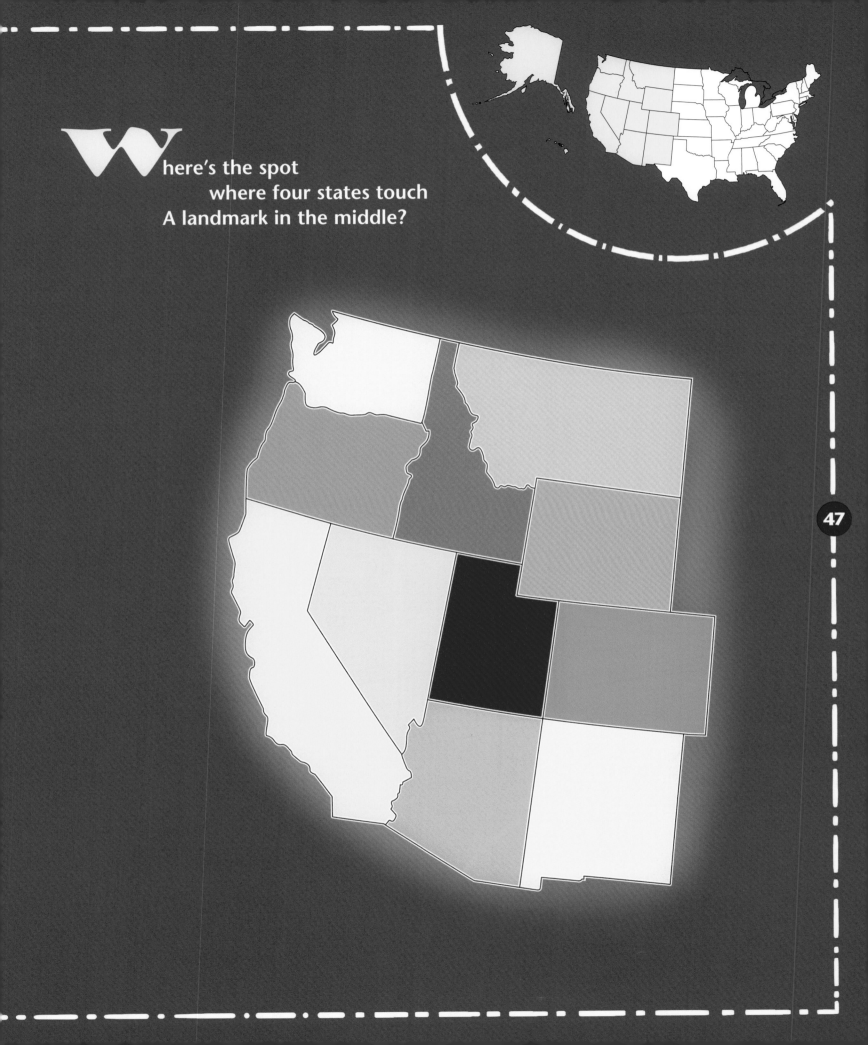

Where's the spot
where four states touch
A landmark in the middle?

Four Corners Navajo Tribal Park!
That's where we go to stand
And spread our fingers
    four states wide,
With just a single hand.

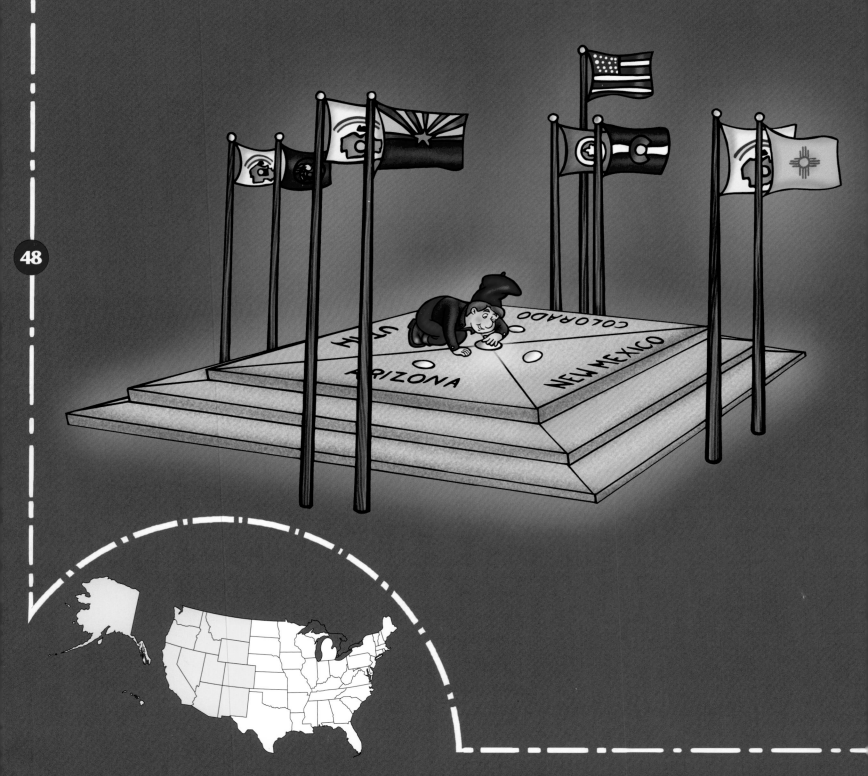

Utah, Colorado form
The top part of a square.
Arizona's just below,
New Mexico its pair.

To learn those states,
        just know UCAN.
Those letters
        spell a clue:
Put U and C
        on A and N,
And UCAN do it too!

A spooky head above UCAN
Is always facing west.
Montana's forehead,
    nose, and chin
Could pass the
    monster
    test!

That head is on a magic block—
Wyoming is the one!
It makes Montana laugh and sing
And have a lot of fun.

They call themselves
    the MoWy Act,
And when
    they come alive,
They entertain
    the other states
By doing MoWy jive.

Montana faces Idaho.
What is it staring at?
An elf complete with turned-up nose
And chimney-patterned hat.

You know that if he could, that elf
Would love to take a swim,
But Washington and Oregon
Sit tight and block him in.

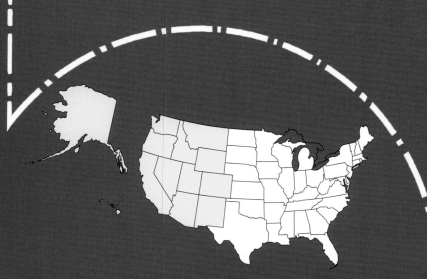

Those two states are 'elf-guards.'
Their devotion is terrific;
They keep the elf from turning 'round
To jump in the Pacific.

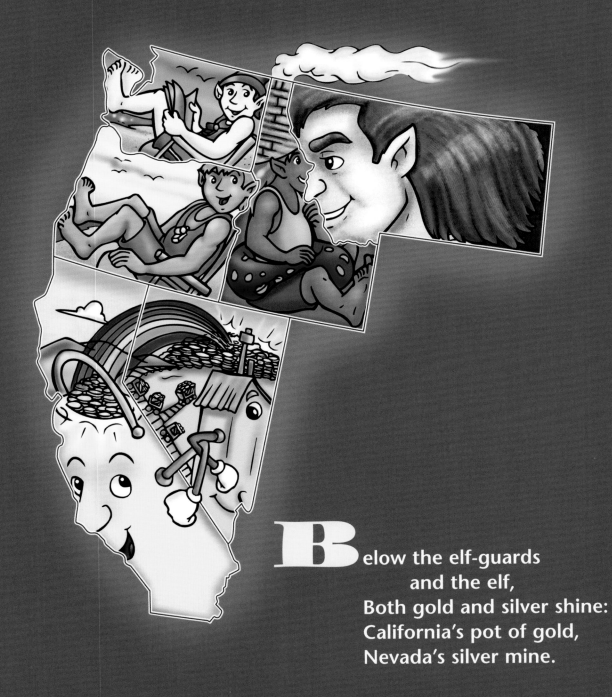

Below the elf-guards
and the elf,
Both gold and silver shine:
California's pot of gold,
Nevada's silver mine.

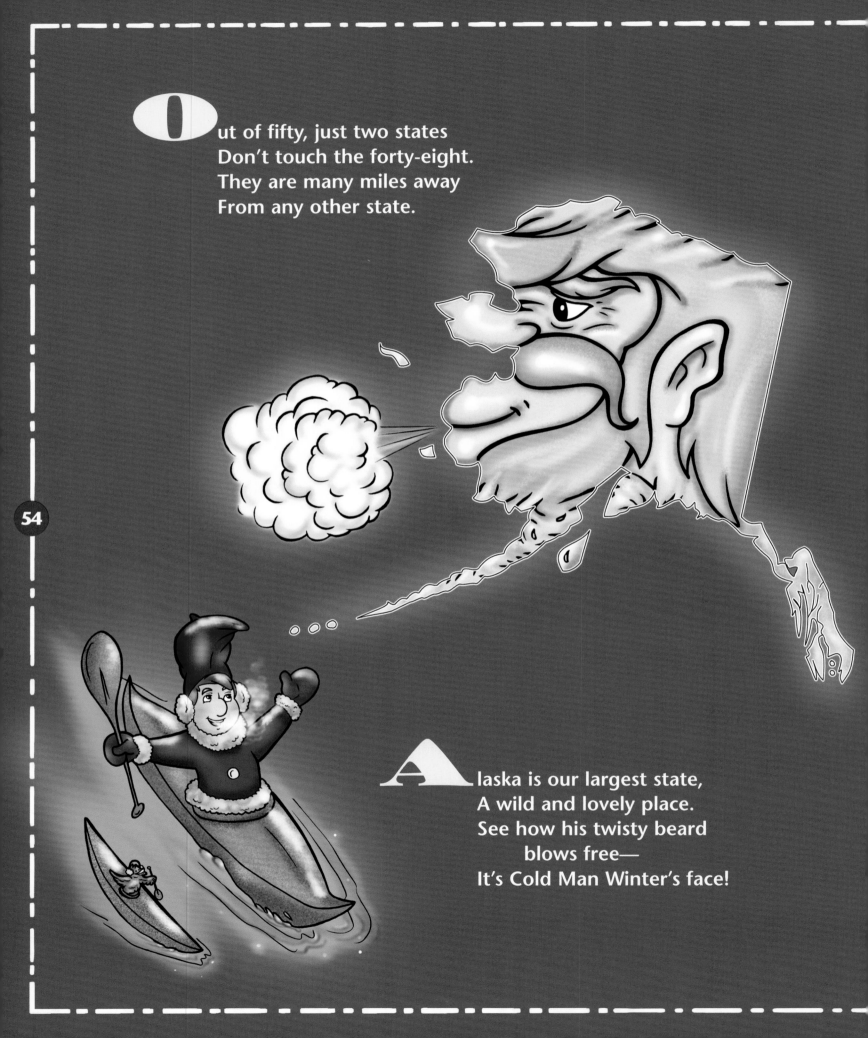

Out of fifty, just two states
Don't touch the forty-eight.
They are many miles away
From any other state.

54

Alaska is our largest state,
A wild and lovely place.
See how his twisty beard
      blows free—
It's Cold Man Winter's face!

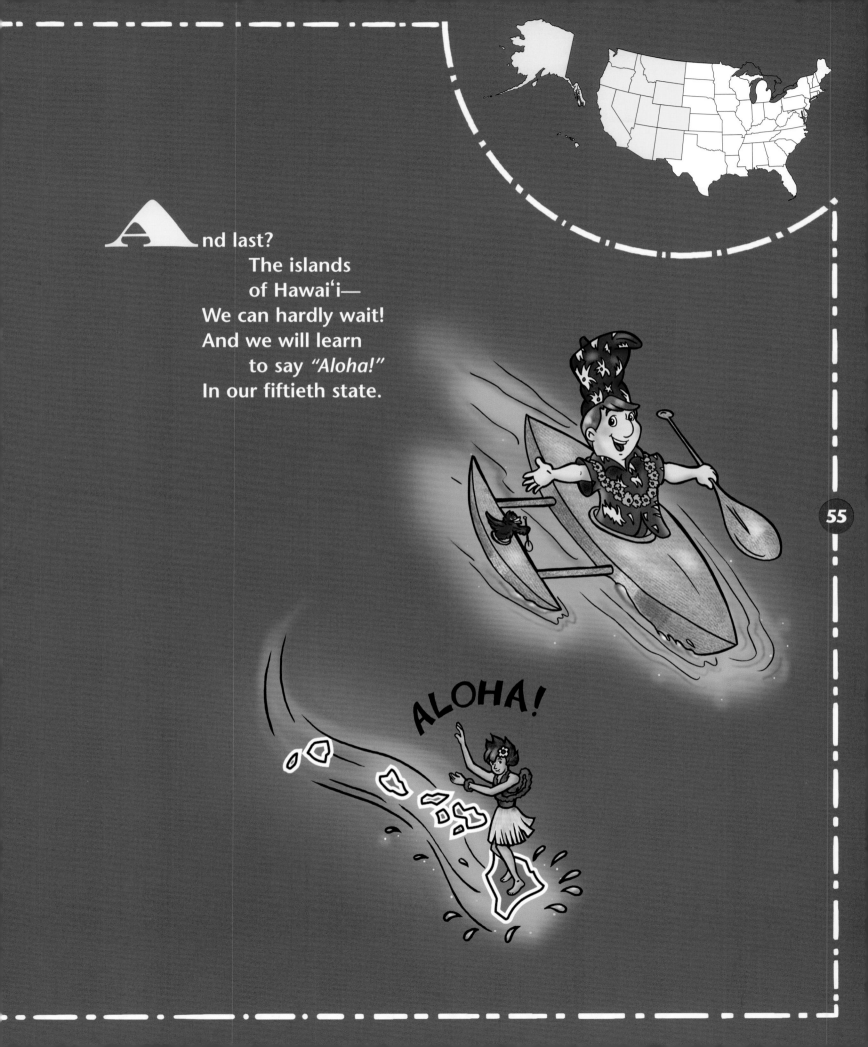

And last?
The islands
of Hawai'i—
We can hardly wait!
And we will learn
to say *"Aloha!"*
In our fiftieth state.

ALOHA!

Western States

13 states

ALOHA!

UCAN, MoWy,
    chimney elf
(Whose elf-guards
    stop his swim).
Aloha, cold face,
    gold and silver...

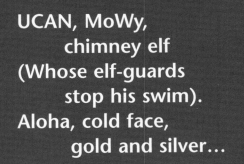

Thanks for

helping, MIM!

60

ALOHA!

The wall map of United States—showing the Little Man In the Map
and all his friends—is available at www.schoolsidepress.com

United States of America

with the Little Man In the Map and friends

"A blank map of the U.S.A.
Plus your imagination
Are all you need
        to learn the states—
All fifty in our nation."

The Little Man In the Map

United States of America

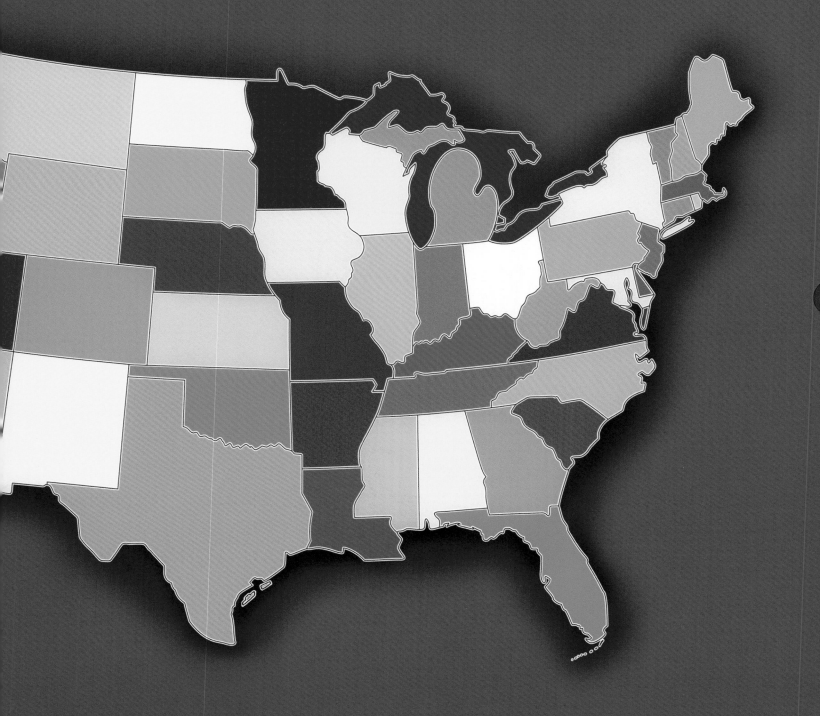